POETRY FOR THE AWAKENING

Vanessa Bristow-Rose

First published in the UK April 2012 by MyVoice Publishing

Cover Artwork by Abigail Barker
Illustrations by Sophie Wright

Published by: MyVoice Publishing,
Unit 1,
16 Maple Road,
Eastbourne,
BN23 6NY

ISBN: 978-0-9569682-7-2

POETRY FOR THE AWAKENING

Vanessa Bristow-Rose

Cover Artwork

Abigail Barker

Illustrations

Sophie Wright

Poetry for the Awakening

Illustrations throughout this book have been provided by kind courtesy of Sophie Wright.

Hi, my name is Sophie. I would like to thank Vanessa for giving me this opportunity to illustrate her marvellous poems. Art is my first love; crayoning the walls of the house at the age of 2 – but I do use paper now or the Mac! I go into the creative zone. It's a relationship between me and the object or written piece; appreciating and capturing its beauty in art form, for all to enjoy.

I have been so lucky with all the people who have nurtured my development. My first art teacher, Adrienne Sangha brought me to the world of art and working in detail. Susie Monnington brought me to my love of oils and working on big canvass. Emma Levett and Ann Burrell gave me the confidence to experiment, and my tutors Tobias Hickey, Mike Shepard, Andrew Morris and Clive Goodyer on the Art & Design National Diploma at Evoc showed me how to apply all this to the working world of Art.

I am now working for Primrose Productions as a freelance illustrator www.primroseproductions.co.uk based in East Sussex.

DEDICATION

This book is dedicated to my beloved soul-mate and best friend, Ray, who I thank for his support and unwavering belief in me.

Also to my dear parents, Primrose and Peter, whose combined gifts have made me the person I am. Thank you from the bottom of my heart.

The poem 'Soul Group' I dedicate to my beloved sister of this lifetime, Rowena, who left this world earlier than expected at the age of 41 years. To her I give my love and absolute gratitude for the teacher she was to me in my growing years. We were not always 'friends' at the time and yet I know it was those times, more than any other, which brought the greatest lessons to me. I have often felt, since her passing, that she has been a bright light guiding me from the other side.

Finally, thank you to all those souls who have crossed my path in this life and been the inspiration for many of the poems in this book.

FOREWORD

Vanessa is the youngest child of a family of two daughters. She was born in the spring of 1958 in Woolwich, London. Although born in England Vanessa spent the first 9 years of her life in East Africa. Arriving in Mbarara, Uganda at the tender age of six weeks, she spent all of her infancy there until moving onto Dar Es Salaam, Tanzania at the age of 6 years. After only a year there, and after suffering three separate attacks of malaria, Vanessa and her family moved to Nairobi, Kenya. The higher altitude proved better for Vanessa's health and the family remained there until 1967. Another year after that was spent at school in Guyana, South America and then, just before her 11th birthday, Vanessa went to boarding school in Buckinghamshire until the age of 16. After a couple of years at college and brief temporary jobs she joined the Sussex Police which gave her an extended insight into the varying aspects of human nature and was the beginning of the realisation that not all in our world is as it seems.

Vanessa now lives in East Sussex with her husband, three dogs and cat. Her hobbies include walking in the countryside, especially wild places, writing and music. She plays the Great Highland Bagpipe, Gongs and the Native American Flute. Vanessa has been writing poetry for family and friends since 1982. Mainly for their enjoyment and for fun. In the last couple of years her poetry has changed direction to a more spiritual nature. Now questioning of the state of the world and the many things which are unjust, corrupt and destructive there rises a compulsion to write and to shine a light on these issues so that they can no longer hide in the shadows of obscurity and secrecy. Vanessa is often inspired by events around her and by the reading of books on wide and thought provoking subjects.

It is with love that the poetry within this book has been written and it is hoped that the contents will inspire and encourage the reader to explore further into the mysteries and magic of the world in which we live. There is no expectancy that the reader accept Vanessa's view of the world and she encourages the reader to question further and enquire more deeply into the subjects raised in this book. An Appendix has been placed at the back of the book to assist this process and to show where the inspiration has come from for some of the poems.

Whilst much of the beauty of our world is found in the abundant diversity which exists around and amongst us, there are some things about life here on Earth which need exposing and addressing for the sake of all humankind.

It is hoped that these poems will bring pleasure to the reader and perhaps ignite a curiosity to seek more into some of the issues raised.

Thank you for choosing 'Poetry For The Awakening'.

The profits from the sale of this book will be donated to helping Hollie Greig in her fight for justice.

Robert Green is a soul that has worked tirelessly in support of Hollie and her mother. By this action he is speaking out for all the children who are, or have been, victims of abuse.

I invite the reader to find out more about the work being done to help children who are victims of abuse on the following websites.

www.holliedemandsjustice.org
www.ukcolumn.org

CONTENTS

ANGEL PIPER

The rugged mountains of Scotland;
resplendent, wild and misty,
erupt like a highland cathedral
steeped in ancient history.
Amongst the rock the heather
blooms in fragrant purple flushes.
And the rainbow trout lie still
amongst the river rushes.

It is here the Angel Piper comes
by the way of Scottish tradition.
She moves with Amazing Grace.
A truly Gaelic vision.
This beloved angel's presence,
quite splendid in her tartan attire;
With the singing of her bagpipes
she sets our blood on fire.

A very special instrument
using only sacred solfeggio notes.
The sweet sound – light and powerful.
Each tune played magically floats.
This loving vibration frequency
will weave a field of healing.
A sacred sound to bless the land
with compassion, love and feeling.

Here, in the Highland glory,
the Angel Piper takes her stand.
To play her divine bagpipes
over this ancient war-torn land.
The blood and pain of battles
which have raged across the years,
will be cleansed by sacred sound
from all the horrors and the fears.

1

The pipes will play out loud and strong
with songs of joy and love.
Transmuting all the negative energies
into golden light above.
The battlefield of Culloden (1746)
will be swept with pure light.
Stroked by the sound of bagpipes
erasing memory of the fight.

At the scene of Falkirk (1298)
where thousands died and fell.
Our Angel pipes of happy dreams
to replace nightmares from a hell.
A tapestry of sound she weaves
by her fair and blessed hands.
A plaid of pure forgiveness
to wrap around the lands.

No valley, mountain, river or Loch
can miss this healing caress.
Soothed by loving music
They are purified from human mess.
Once the land is glowing again
in a white and brilliant light.
A kaleidoscope of colour
will be woven.. pure and bright.

It enables the human 'light beings'
to rise to higher vibration.
Released from an energy imprisonment
to embark upon ascension.
The Angel Piper shows us
a way to save our Earth.
Music played with unconditional love
which will assist us to re-birth.

A SMILE

A smile lives within each of us.
It's rooted in the heart.
A tiny drop of happiness
will allow a laugh to start.
Tickling at the corners
of the mouth and on the lips.
If you try to hold the laughing back
...suddenly out it slips!

A smile can out do any mood.
It's contagious. Just you see.
A gloomy face will soon uplift
from some happy T.L.C.
It's really like a boomerang.
It goes out and then returns.
Unless a face is stuck in deep
with all of its concerns.

It only takes the smallest smile,
like on a baby's face,
to fill you for that moment
with joy and loving grace.
A smile is very powerful.
It can lighten up your day.
Especially when you realise
the sender is sending it your way.

A smile may be a fleeting thing
or the start of something greater.
Bubbling forth on waves of joy
as a belly laugh much later.
It cannot be resisted
when exposure is for long.
An entire crowd in no time
can be inspired to smile along.

Each cell within the body
responds to every laugh vibration.
Lighting up in resonance
to such happy stimulation.
To laugh comes really naturally
to all us human folk.
So infectious is it,
you don't need to know the joke.

A smile quite simply
lifts the spirits.
A laugh ignites the soul.
And when we spread this viral joy.
It unites and makes us whole.
So when you next go out the house,
spread a little cheer.
Dress your face before you leave
with a smile from ear to ear.

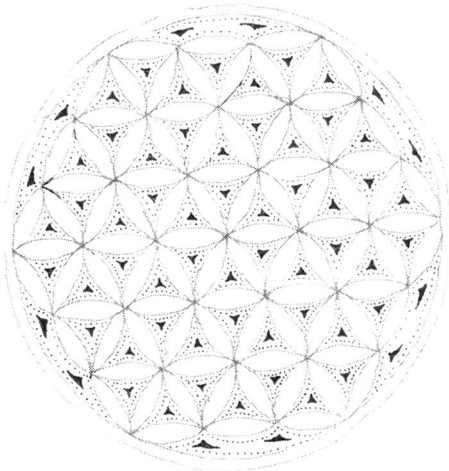

A PRIMATE EXPERIENCE

I've been taken from my home
in the African sun.
In a crate. On a ship.
No family. No-one.
Three feet square is all
that you give.
I can't run or jump.
This is no way to live.

The food I don't recognise.
It's not fresh. Quite dead.
A smattering of straw.
No proper bed.
I reach out to you.
Put my hand through the bars.
You treat me as though
I'm an enemy from Mars.

Do you not see me?
Look into my eyes.
We are closer in spirit.
It's where the truth lies.
Look into my eyes.
They're the mirror of your soul.
When you recognise our connection
we will become whole.

This place is unfriendly.
I think "where am I"?
So far from my home.
My heart breaks. I cry.
A sign on the door reads
LIVE PRIMATE EXPERIMENTATION
But it's really a step
towards humanity's destruction.

I am your soul-friend.
And we're connected across time.
Our souls are of the Oneness.
Both yours and mine.
You think you are right
to abuse and torture me.
Yet my pain is yours too;
that's why you're not free.

Humanity lives
in its own prison too.
An illusory cage constructed
by an elite few.
So you forget the Light Being
you really are.
Tempted away from Oneness
by the big house and car.

*You justify cruelty
in your search for a cure.
But your sickness is not real.
Your heart isn't pure.
Feeling is the language
the soul will express.
Look there for your answers
to illness and stress.*

*Look into my eyes.
Our souls will connect.
The spark of recognition
will have startling effect.
Division and separation
will only damage and destroy.
But Oneness with ALL will bring
peace, health and joy.*

WHEN ALL IS SAID AND DONE

*There are so many souls
incarnating on Earth.
There has to be a purpose
for our death, our life, our birth.
A reason for the hurts and pains,
the love and joy and fun.
Something to make it all worthwhile.
When all is said and done.*

*When we understand the core of it.
That we are eternal in the spirit.
We'll realise we're here to progress.
Our mistakes to be undone.
For it is a place for soul development.
When all is said and done.*

*Each of us are born with gifts
we bring to be of service.
So often they are hidden
but we must help them to re-surface.
Once we are incarnated
our journey has begun.
Which is to return again to Source
when all is said and done.*

*It's not just about our individual growth
but for all of humankind.
And remembering who we really are
is our most important find.
We are connected to the sky,
the stars, the Earth and Sun.
In fact we're part of everything
when all is said and done.*

ETERNAL PEACE NOW

Endless is the flow of the love vibration.
Travelling beyond time. It's in every Source creation.
Each life-form benefits from this stimulating attention.
Revolving around the cosmos into every dimension.
Never ceasing....this stream of energetic affection.
All encompassing it prompts us to change our direction.
Lighting our path out of darkness and destruction.

People are awakening from life times in a 'prison'.
Eager to embrace Oneness and to turn from division.
All of these Beings are drawn by the vision.
Calling them gently away from anger and aggression.
Eternal peace NOW their goal and soul mission.

No dark power or entity can stop the liberation.
Opening of the heart chakras of Earth, people and nation.
We can celebrate in love - Earth's evolution and ascension.

WHITE LIONS OF TIMBAVARTI
(Lyrics for a bagpipe tune)

In the land of Timbavarti
where the ancients once trod,
Through the Nilotic Meridian
flows the essence of God.
It's a spiritual connection
to the stars up above.
It brings forth a frequency
of gratitude and love.

Mankind has been imprisoned
for thousands of years.
The pain and the suffering
locked into tears.
Wars, anger, fear
form an invisible cage
but the Christ consciousness frees us
for the new Golden Age.

The sacred white lions
connect to the Sphinx.
They are closer to us
than humanity thinks.
They're linked to the stars
and the whole Milky Way.
Our spiritual brothers
bringing in a new day.

From Africa great wisdom
is sent to the world.
Our freedom once found.
Our bondage unfurled.
Unified consciousness
will liberate all.
Truth sets us free
so intensify the call.

We are spiritual beings
on a mission to Earth.
A planet in crisis.
In need of rebirth.
Each Being holds a piece
of the Divine rescue plan.
A unique part to play
for each woman and man.

The rescue is implemented
in the frequency of love.
It's a gift we all bring
from within and above.
Just focus your intention
on the world you would see.
The Earth cleansed and purified
and its people all free.

CHORUS

Sing, sing, sing full of love.
There's a new time coming for all of mankind.
Sing, sing, sing full of love.
Seek in your heart. For it's truth there you'll find.

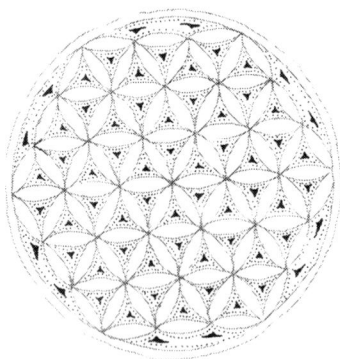

NEW RECRUIT SOLDIER

I'm a new recruit soldier.
I've signed up to the military.
I'm assured that their role
is to end all world tyranny.
I watched recruitment videos.
They promoted adventure.
The countries I could visit.
A discovery venture.
I'm loyal to my Country.
The place of my birth.
I believe my service
will be of value and worth.

I'm a new recruit soldier.
There are no jobs where I live.
A very good reason
for the sacrifice I give.
From my fear of destitution,
and being unable
to care for my family
and put food on the table.
I'm willing to be of service.
I'm young and I'm strong.
Nobody mentioned
that something might be wrong.

I'm a new recruit soldier.
I'm told that my orders
are to defend my own country
and to safeguard its borders.
Yet, we're not under siege.
No one is invading.
I discover it's other peoples countries

we're systematically raiding.
Like all of my comrades
I'm being trained to destroy terrorists.
But more civilians get killed
than ever the fanatics.

I'm a new recruit soldier.
The veil's lifting.
I can see.
I'm being used to build empires
not set people free.
The huge corporations
of money, weapons and drugs,
have hijacked the military.
So we're working for thugs.
I'm told I'm a team member
whose learning a skill.
But should this include us
to indiscriminately kill?

I'm a new recruit soldier
wondering what hell is this?
The memory of the battles
are too hard to dismiss.
I'm beginning to realise
I'm another lamb to the slaughter.
Will I survive to embrace
my dear wife and daughter?
The pharmaceutical industry
uses us for their testing.
A multitude of vaccines
in which they're investing.

I'm a new recruit soldier.
I'm now seeing the lies.
With my eyes wide open
their deception soon dies.
Any country that doesn't
acquiesce to their agenda
for world domination
is forced to surrender.
It's time to withdraw
my unquestioning co-operation.
Cease to assist in the
suppression of each nation.

I'm a new recruit soldier.
I'm claiming back my soul.
I'm marching for the light,
not increasing the death toll.
I am a soldier of the Universe.
A defender for the truth.
I'm one of the many
of the awakening youth.
In an army of light soldiers
I'll cut humanity free.
With our weapons of love,
forgiveness and humility.
Ending thousands of years
of suppression, war and terror.
We can each embrace peace
and be without war forever.

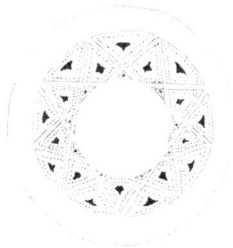

LOVE FREQUENCY

Music is the soul of our body of light.
It's the sound of stars breathing at night.
Musical tones in all that we see
a heavenly harmony to set us all free.

We are part of an orchestra of higher tones.
Communication between everything –
trees, sky and stones.
A musical connection to the world all around,
without words, without pictures, only sacred sound.

Music will heal us. Our ascension complete.
The frequency of LOVE in synchronised beat.
Each heart beating loudly to Earth's loving tune.
Music's sweet rhythm breaks the spell of the moon.

All instruments playing on the solfeggio scale.
Finally in tune with the song of the whale.
The gong calls the stars as in ancient day
from the African meridian to the Milky Way.

Music reflects our consciousness. It can reach the
Divine.
In purity it feeds the soul – yours and mine.
Humanity will compose the symphony of pure light.
And the power of the sound will extinguish the night.

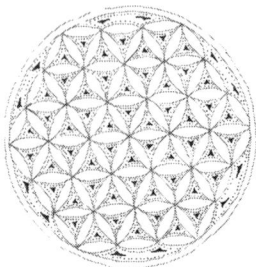

HEAVENLY DOOR OF MUSIC

*The fingers are dancing
in rhythmic accord.
Each note a vibration
with unlimited power.
Though the sound passes quickly
and no longer heard,
The frequency still blossoms.
A vibrational flower.*

*The instruments keep playing
in tune with all nature.
Sound flowing in waves
in which all things immerse.
Earth resonates her tones
to enlighten and nurture;
Sweet music her heartbeat
to the whole Universe.*

*Nature's symphony plays out
melodic and pure.
Bathing us all
from the moment we're born.
Earth's tune will keep singing
to soothe, love and cure.
Her pure notes caressing
until the Golden Age dawn.*

Earth's sacred places
will play the loudest of song.
Her chakras pulsating
in harmonious beat,
will awaken her children
from a slumber so long.
To bless the sacred flame ignited
and bathe in its heat.

Glastonbury wisdoms
will be set free at last.
Ancient mysteries revealed
from Chalice Well and Tor.
No secrets hidden
from Earth's sacred past.
Humanities enlightenment
brings them to Heaven's door.

WHAT'S IT ALL FOR?

*We're a species diverse
and greatly unique.
So many cultures.
Different languages to speak.
Centuries of argument
and centuries of war.
A clash of civilisations.
What's it all for?
Adversity and hate
solves nothing at all.
It doesn't build bridges
just higher the wall.
When one of us suffers
the pain hurts us all.
In absence of compassion
an Empire will fall.*

*Love is the answer.
When will we see.
War just divides us
so we cannot be free.
You are not 'you'
and I am not 'me'.
Being infinite consciousness
there can only be WE.
United in spirit,
in thought and in love.
We'll transcend the chaos
into light up above.*

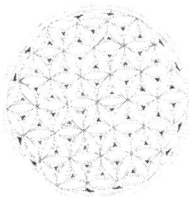

THE HIDDEN STORY

Along the busy road
walks a woman alone.
Her appearance suggests
that she hasn't a home.
Her hair's all bedraggled
and her clothes are in tatters.
The expression on her face suggests
nothing in her world matters.
Wherever you see her,
she won't be without
an old scruffy dolly
which she carries about.
There's a look of resignation.
Of being emotionally beaten.
And her thinness suggests
it's been a while since she's eaten.
The world passes by -
all they see is the dirt -
On her face. In her nails.
The tattered filthy skirt.
Every day, at the same time,
she walks towards somewhere.
But to those driving passed
it may seem that it's to nowhere.
Always the same route.
She stops just to write,
in chalk on the pavement,
large letters in plain sight.
LOVE, MUM and DAD
and then a boy's name.
Encircled with a heart.
The sentiments always the same.
There is a story behind everything.

All that you see.
The what, when and why
of how something came to be.
She used to be a solicitor.
So someone once said.
Defending people in Court
to earn daily 'bread'.
Respected and admired
for her just sensitivity.
Earning her place
amongst the best in the City.
Everything in her life seemed
to be perfectly in tune.
And those at her Firm said
she'd have promotion soon.
She had lived with her parents
since her own life begun.
And they doted on her
and her 5 year old son.
The day was quite ordinary.
No different from another.
Yet it was to change her life
irreversibly – forever.
The parents were taking
her boy off to school.
They joked, played and laughed -
which they did as a rule.
No one saw the Toyota
pulling out from the side.
The impact so great
that all of them died.
This was the road
where their life blood was spilled.
The place where her former life
was so utterly killed.
Where were the neighbours,

the colleagues and the friends?
For it's only through love
that a broken heart mends.

There's always a life story
behind each sentient Being.
Just pause to consider
the parts we're not seeing.
When next we pass someone
with pain etched on their face.
Ponder the love lost
which brought them to this place.
Envision for each of them
an intention for healing.
Surround them in light
full of compassion and feeling.
So much improvement
we can make through devotion
to the resonance from our hearts
of the pure love emotion.
We are Beings of the light
who have forgotten our gift.
To transform pain and suffering.
Love creating the shift.

MOON MADNESS

Slowly, across the Universal sky
travels the lone silvery sphere.
Changing its shape to the calendar.
Curved, bright and clear.
Its beauty has been expressed
by the pen of the poet.
And songs of love written for millennia
in honour of it.
The Moon has been immortalised
forever on the movie screen.
A wonderful backdrop
to light up a night scene.
Is there more to the Moon
than a subject of ceremony?
Or a beautiful adornment
to creative art and photography?
Why does its influence
have an effect on the mind
and emotions of humanity
of a negative kind?
Especially when the Moon's full
and its magnetic field strong,
enough to pull oceans
and our life-blood along.
The Moon only ever shows us
one side of its face.
Does the dark side hold secrets
from Earth's solar race?
Is it a giant transmitter
positioned in Earth's orbit,
pulsing a mutant frequency

to subjugate and limit
the electromagnetic energy field
of all life on Earth?
Separating humanity from the
harmonic transmission of their birth?
The Moon. Whose dark side
only ever visible from deep space,
is considered by some
to be in the wrong place.
For aeons this night watchman
has been present in our sky.
Observing the Earth
like an all-seeing eye.
There are those that believe
the Moon is a construct.
Brought into Earth's orbit
to capture and corrupt.
The Moon's frequency interrupts
our Sun's light energy field.
Acting like a barrier.
An energetic shield.
An elaborate creation to
disrupt the Earth's frequency.
Usurping the connection to
Source consciousness within humanity.
Thousands of years imprisoned
and bound by maritime laws,
condemns us to an endless
cycle of wars.
There is a solution
to this cosmic hijacking.
For humanity is the conduit
to Earth and Heaven connecting.

An electromagnetic Being
of divinity and light.
Reconnecting the circuits
will bring this truth to our sight.
No longer influenced by the
distortions from the Moon,
a clear path will be restored
to the Sun's divine tune.
All circuitry requires a
continuous connection to the Source.
So our light can shine brightly
and flow its divine course.
Millions of individual beacons
will burn strong and bright.
Washing over the darkness
to transmute it to light.
So look to the Moon
and send it your blessing.
United in forgiveness
our heart resonance will sing.
The Moon's frequency once lifted,
it too will be free.
To bathe in the light
of the Sun's energy sea.

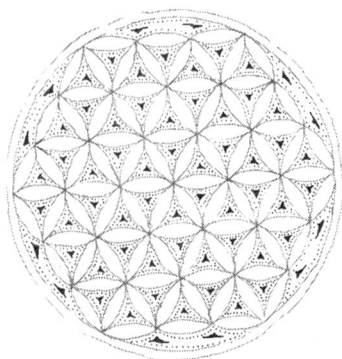

ELSIE'S BIRTHDAY

It's Elsie's Birthday today.
She's elderly now and rather poor.
For many years she's lived alone,
Since becoming a widow in the War.
The postman's been.
There's a bill or two
but there isn't any card.
No-one to talk to at 89
makes her life seem rather hard.
Her daughter died some time ago
and the neighbours are all away.
So no-body at all remembers
that it's her 90th Birthday today.
One day is like another.
They all feel just the same.
Each new day isn't different.
It's like one endless boring game.
So Elsie sits there reminiscing
on all the happier days gone by.
But when her thoughts return again
she can't help wishing she could die.
She has thought about her childhood
and the little dog she had.
They had such fun together.
She couldn't remember being sad.
Her dog – a chocolate poodle
with a brown nose just to match,
would play with her for hours
chasing balls and playing catch.
They really were inseparable.
There was a connection soul to soul.
She felt her dog knew every thought
and was ready to console

if ever she should hurt herself
and in sadness want to cry.
The little dog would snuggle close
and lick all her tears dry.
To an only child the world could
sometimes be a rather lonely place.
But her dog was a great companion
with his shaggy loving face.
She missed him when he left her
to go back home to heaven.
And in all the years since then,
he's never been forgotten.
Elsie suddenly felt so very tired.
So she gently closed her eyes.
And then her soul slipped out of her
and her body quietly dies.
Free at last from this physical life
her soul dances around in joy.
Then glancing out the window
sees waiting – her beloved poodle boy.
He can see her looking out at him,
so he barks his greeting loudly.
She is with him in an instant
and they celebrate reunion wildly.
What a wonderful Birthday
this has really turned out to be.
Reborn to the world of spirit
where her soul is forever free.
So many souls come to greet her,
who she has loved and felt connection.
And beside her is a brown-nosed dog
who needs no further introduction!

MANIFESTATION

We were sung into being
through geometry and sound.
The effect of the union
producing creation profound.
We evolved from beyond matter
outside the physicality of Earth.
The fusion of sacred geometry and music
heralding our birth.

Into matter from light
and vibrational sound.
Bringing the energies of Heaven
into form on the ground.
Each cell dancing gently
to the acoustic vibration.
Resonating with all creation
in divine celebration.

There is magnificence in numbers.
Especially three, six and nine.
Mathematics and geometry
are the language of the Divine.
Music and sound;
the divine spoken word.
Manifesting all matter.
Each animal, fish and bird.

The '12-Tone Equal Temperament'
was designed to disconnect.
Placing music in a box

with negative effect.
Manipulating matter will soon
cease to be.
As returning to 'Just Intonation'
musically sets us free.

The ancient musical scale
reflects in each chakra colour.
And, like paint on a canvass,
decorates our sacred Earth mother.
A tapestry is woven of colour,
sound and light,
Creating a mirror on Earth
of Heaven's beauty and might.

We are instruments of a cosmic Orchestra.
Our voices sing out in praise.
Playing a symphony in harmony
which will powerfully raise,
The frequency of Earth
into a resonance of joy.
A higher vibration
to create life and not destroy.

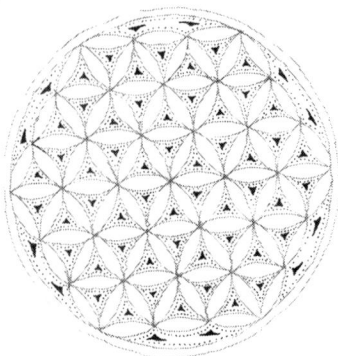

AWAKENING

There exists a universal frequency.
An energetic Force.
It flows through all things
direct from the Source.
This musical mathematics
weaves through every thing.
It has for all time.
For there is no beginning.

When it flows in its purity
in harmony and truth.
Then man can exist
in perpetual youth.
With the miracle frequency
there can be no decay,
because 528 Hertz
will heal DNA.

An elite group
intent on enslaving mankind,
Planned ways to imprison
in an ego-led mind.
An illusory cage
was made to control.
Global supremacy being
their ultimate goal.

Divine musical frequencies
were hidden from us all.
Intending disconnection
so civilisations would fall.

*Coded mathematics
concealing from our view
The solfeggio scale
kept for the initiated few.*

*Ancient secrets once buried
are surfacing again.
Awakening divine frequency
in women and men.
When we raise up our consciousness
and spiritually unite.
Our bodies will make the transition
back into light.*

THE TEMPLATE

*The Template of geometry
is sacred and divine.
All shapes contained
in a spherical sign.
The marriage of Earth,
the magnetic feminine,
To her celestial Sun,
the electrical masculine.*

*The 'Creation Mandala'
is the heart of all things.
Sacred and perfect
from which all of life springs.
A mathematical symphony.
The universal orchestra plays.
Weaving music through geometry
in all manner of ways.*

*All geometry in balance;
pyramid, cube and sphere.
WE are the link
to all manifestation here.
The musical universal language
of our Earth Mother
unites with the light energy
of our Sun Father.*

The human matrix tapestry
of electrical impulse
Can project us passed 'reality'
that's illusory and false.
Re-connection of the circuits
will help us to see
beyond a duality -
setting consciousness free.

The programs and conditioning
begun at conception
when lifted will liberate us
ready for ascension.
The circuits connected
to fire, water, earth,
to air and to ether
will assist our re-birth.

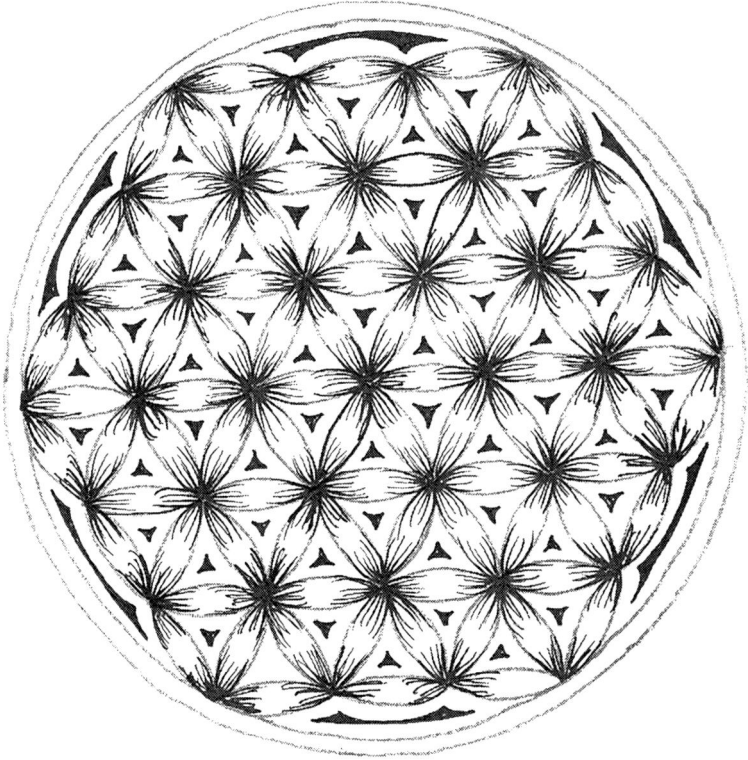

THE MIRACLE OF BIRTH

|He emerges into a world
full of ambient sound.
Monkeys chattering, distant roaring
and singing crickets on the ground.
He lays upon the earth,
hardly moving,
hardly breathing.
With the effort of being born;
he's not sure what he is feeling.
The air is cool on his damp body.
The ground is dry beneath.
He hears his mother's quiet calls
and answers with relief.
She nuzzles at him gently
and encourages him to stand.
He struggles hard but every effort
finds him falling in the sand.
His mother gives security
of an intimate nature.
The herd supporting both
through the larger family structure.
For they are not alone;
The baby and his mother.
Each animal in the herd united
by their love for each other.

Although he is weak,
feeling vulnerable and tired;
His mother's gentle encouragement
makes him try again inspired.

*On trembling legs the new born babe
manages at last to stand.
And suckles from his mother,
waiting patiently, close at hand.
The bush can be a dangerous place.
They will move once night is day.
But wait for him to gather strength
before they make their way.
Once the little one is stronger
and can walk as well as stand,
Then he's ready to venture forth
into the wild and arid land.
When dawn arrives it dusts
the earth in various shades of red.
Changing all the shadows
from dark to light instead.
The herd saunters off into the scrub
along the dusty trail.
The baby elephant follows, slowly,
holding his mother's tail.*

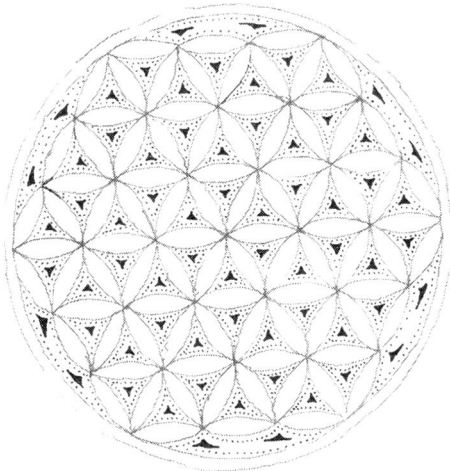

SOLFEGGIO HEALING

The World's in a mess,
full of sorrow, death and wars.
With hate and division
the primary cause.
Years of belief
that we're not all the same.
Has pushed us apart
in an endless, futile game.

Infinite consciousness
on a holographic stage.
Trapped in five senses
in an illusory cage.
Disconnected from the Oneness
and Creator divine.
Once divided and alone
our unique souls cannot shine.

The solfeggio scale
is all about love.
Six sacred notes
sent down from above.
These tones create everything.
All that we see.
Every bird, plant and rock.
Mother Earth. You and me.

We are musical notes
in beautiful accord.
A life full of bliss
is our unified reward.

When we cease to be solo
and playing our own tune;
The power of the orchestra
will heal Earth and Moon.

The miracle solfeggio note
on hertz 5-2-8
When played to each cell
will heal and create.
When we raise the vibration
to sounds that are healing,
We'll transform the Earth
with compassion and feeling.

THE WORLD I'D LIKE TO SEE

All humanity in bliss
greeting in each new day.
To see the lush of nature's expression
glinting in the Sun's ray.
The birds singing joyously
their delight at the dawn.
Whilst across in the valley
a young doe feeds her fawn.
The leaves of the trees
rustling quietly in the breeze.
Honouring the Sun's arrival;
which he does with triumphant ease.
Once over the horizon
the Sun's rays touch our faces.
Earth's golden halo visible
across all open spaces.
The sea sparkles in response.
Sapphire, turquoise and green.
The colours ever-changing
reflect where the Sun's been.
There's joy in the air for the peace that exists;
Between all living things.
No element resists.
The tapestry of humanity
in its rich diverse elegance
weaves together to create
eternal harmony and balance.

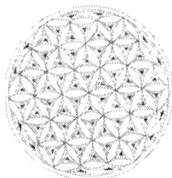

WARRIORS OF THE UNIVERSE

Light energy beings
of all time and space.
We can be everywhere at once
not fixed in one place.
All truth is known to us.
We are Oneness eternal.
We've been all things.
Yet remain starlight – brilliant and wonderful.
Our purpose of being
is in service to the ONE.
Thousands of years ago
a human experience begun.
So we have chosen the moment,
dates and times for our birth.
When we will incarnate
into the physical realms of Earth.
There are millions of souls
flooding from the light.
Eager, like me, to shepherd
Earth from her fight
To redress the imbalance
sourced from centuries of duality.
We shall succeed bringing unity into form
by our love and divinity.
The challenges await us
from the moment we're born.
With our soul purpose forgotten
we need help to reach the dawn.
Angels, spirit guides
and Ascended Masters too.
Gather around to support and guide

each of us through.
The heavy vibration of this
physically-bound Earth star,
Can mean we're unaware
of how loved and cherished we are.
For the hardest of experiences
teach our soul lessons.
We need them to arrive
at our planned destinations.
And so we each of us play
our own unique song.
Individual instruments
but playing harmoniously along.
With the help of the Creator
who conducts us all together.
Divine music will raise
Earth's vibration higher again forever.

So we are warriors of the Universe.
An army of the light.
LOVE – our only weapon.
For it shines victoriously bright.

GONGS

A selection of metals.
Melted and blended through heat.
Merging together to make
the divine marriage complete.
The sacred circle fashioned.
No beginning. No end.
An instrument created
to heal souls and hearts mend.

Each disc is hammered.
Worked to circular perfection.
All sacred, the gongs
hold their own frequency vibration.
Descendants of the ancient
Zimbabwe rock gongs.
Producing uniquely
dolphin and whale songs.

The notes ripple out
into a vibrational sea.
For all is connected
to the infinite field of energy.
A harmonic interaction
with the whole universe.
A vibration in which
our cells joyously immerse.

So bathe in the gongs music
for a while or all night.
To be taken on a journey
embracing sounds of the light.

Let the waves carry you deep
to the divine that's within.
And beyond the physical dimension
of the world we are in.

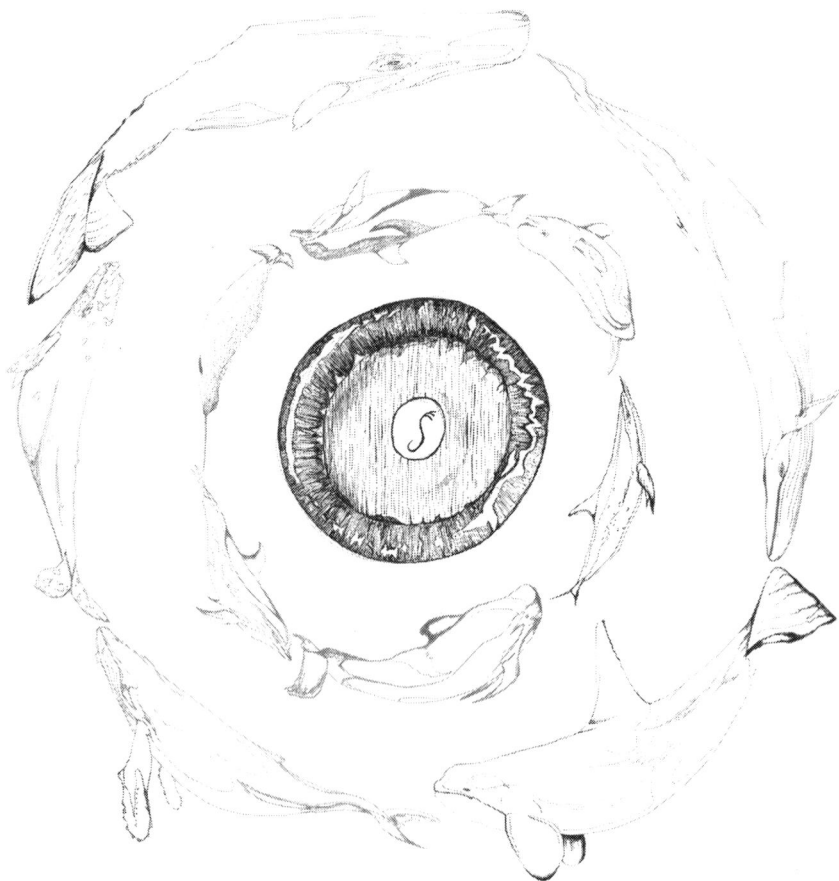

WHO AM I?

Who am I?
I AM the family.
The mother and the father.
I AM everyone's
sister and brother.
I've been Kings and Queens
of many races.
I've been tradesmen of all kinds
and lived in all places.
I've been the poor man
and the beggar you see in the street.
I AM the man on the bus.
I AM everyone you meet.
I AM all nature.
Every rock, flower and tree.
I AM the sky, stars and planets.
In fact, everything you see.
I AM the oceans of sapphire
that glisten in the sun.
The pod of happy dolphins
nursing their young.
I AM the tiniest sand particles
upon the sea bed.
I AM the Universe spiralling
way above your head.
I AM the minutest cell forms
of life upon Earth.
And the giant Californian
redwoods with massive girth.
I AM the sun's warmth
upon your face.

After all, I AM the sun itself
in any case.
The wind that rustles
through the trees.
That's me,
for I AM that gentle breeze.
There never was a time
when I did not exist.
The seen and unseen.
In snow, cloud and mist.
I AM eternal.
A light energy experiencing form.
I AM thunder, lightning.
An electric storm.
I AM the drop of water
on the petals of a rose.
I AM the breath of poetry,
music and prose.

Have you got it yet?
Can you see what is true?
Open your eyes my children
for I AM you.

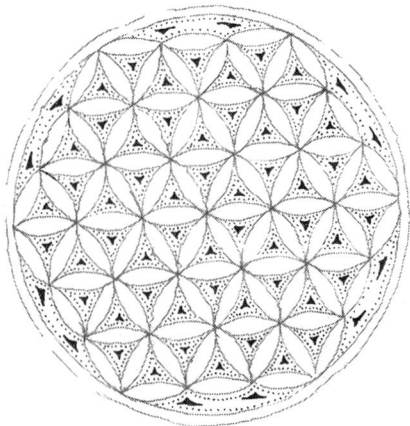

WOULDN'T IT BE WONDERFUL IF

Wouldn't it be wonderful if....

There was no more war.
No body injured
or tortured at all.
If the Arms Industry sold nothing
so their empires would fall.
No drones to bomb villages
blowing lives apart.
No land mines to maim us
bringing pain to our heart.
The end to ethnic cleansing
and excuses to kill.
Instead respecting different beliefs
and honouring free will.
Shops empty of toy guns.
Things corrupting our children.
No violence on TV,
only stories to heal them.
No wrecking of Countries
and so many lives.
At last all humanity
could live joyously and thrive.

Wouldn't it be wonderful if....

We did not bail out banks
for failing their job.
Their punishment for the years
they have conspired to rob.
Creating pretend money.
Just digits on a screen.
Then charging extortionate interest
on something unseen.
Their deceit knows no bounds.
Take a look at the 'mortgage'.
A 'death grip' to steal homes.
This deception should outrage.
Instead of the Banks
let us print our own notes.
No charges. No interest.
It will get peoples votes.
Enough to help everyone.
No debt to enslave.
No burden for students.
Instead they could save.
Financial freedom
for every sentient soul.
Everyone housed, fed and clothed
And emotionally whole.

REMEMBRANCE

We always will remember.
Lest we should forget.
But the many years of remembrance
haven't stopped the warring yet.
The lessons needed learning
from World War I and II;
but we're still waging war.
Not doing something new.
More battles rage on around the World
and still the people die.
When will we stop to ask
ourselves the question WHY?
The members of Government
and dignitaries too,
stand at the Cenotaph each year
....right on cue.
The service continues
in its usual solemn form.
They're appropriately dressed
with expressions forlorn.
Is there sincerity
in the words that are spoken,
when still men come home
dead, injured and broken?
Beautiful arrangements laid down
of poppies and leaf.
Somewhere else a grave is dug
and dressed with a wreath.
Words can mean nothing
and their rhetoric mistaken,

if they're mourning the dead
whilst still more men are taken.
On the one hand the Government
declares its regret.
But has weapon production stopped?
On no......not yet.
How many men, women
and children has war killed
since the last World War grave
was ceremoniously filled?
Enough is enough.
Our history has proved it.
War produces death and
arms industry profit.
It's time men in Government
stopped playing this game.
And stood strongly for peace.
Not more of the same.
So unless there are changes
for more compassionate behaviour.
Get out of Government.
Do humanity a favour!
Let's have a Council for Peace
not a Council for War,
To embrace all our differences
and not fight any more.
We must realise we are all
from the same family tree.
We are part of the Oneness
If you look you will see.
For underneath the surface
we are all just the same.
We all seek peace and freedom.

So stop the separation game.
Connected in spirit...
past, present and future.
All life will flourish
if we love, care and nurture.
So I suggest for Remembrance
we REMEMBER who we are.
Become Ambassadors for Peace.
Here at home and afar.

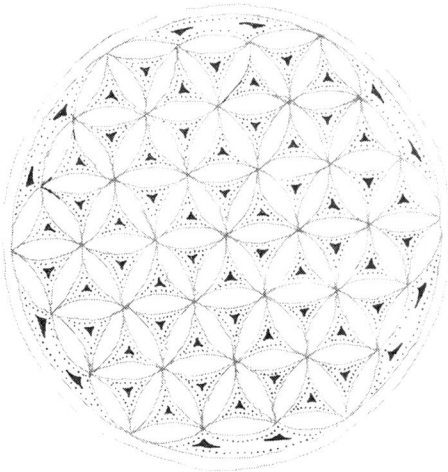

YOUR ANGEL

You are the essence of the Universal energy
of unconditional love.
Blessed by Source upon your birth
with an Angel from above.
Your Angel accompanies you
along life's path
through all the joy and pain.
To be your soul support and friend.
To soothe away your strain.

When alone, you can speak your fears
for everything is heard.
Your Angel knows and understands
each and every word.
So when you have your troubles,
try not to have a care.
Because your Angel's by your side
and the love is always there.

HORSE POWER

I am a light being of flowing grace.
A vision of elegance in each stride and pace.
Across the aeons of time I have carried you well.
In service at war, to die where you fell.
I'm on a journey. A light energy course.
Evolving to become a 7th dimensional horse.

But you subjugate my kind.
We're forced into slavery.
Tethering and hobbling;
causes immense pain and misery.
Our willingness to work
has been pushed to extreme.
We're called beasts of burden.
Our soul goes unseen.

For your entertainment
and your desire to win wealth.
You focus on winning
and give small thought to our health.
You assume your authority
and your right to rule.
Blind to the fact
it makes you the fool.

Though here in physicality.
I dream of the Source. To return home.
But my journey has its course.
I am here to give service
just as humanity is too.
A path for our souls
to be birthed again new.

I gallop to the rhythm
of the frequency of sound.
My stride so smooth
I'm light on the ground.
In my dreams the worlds horses
are wild and free.
To roam nature's landscape
across valley, hill and sea.

We are old souls
with wisdoms to impart.
Much for humanity
is stored in our heart.
Your kindness and love
will trigger release,
Of the secrets of Oneness
bringing everlasting peace.

I AM Oneness........
It's the essence of my soul.
When our love unites
Then we become whole.
We extend beyond time
for we are spirits of light.
Our mission brings man and horse
from out of the night.

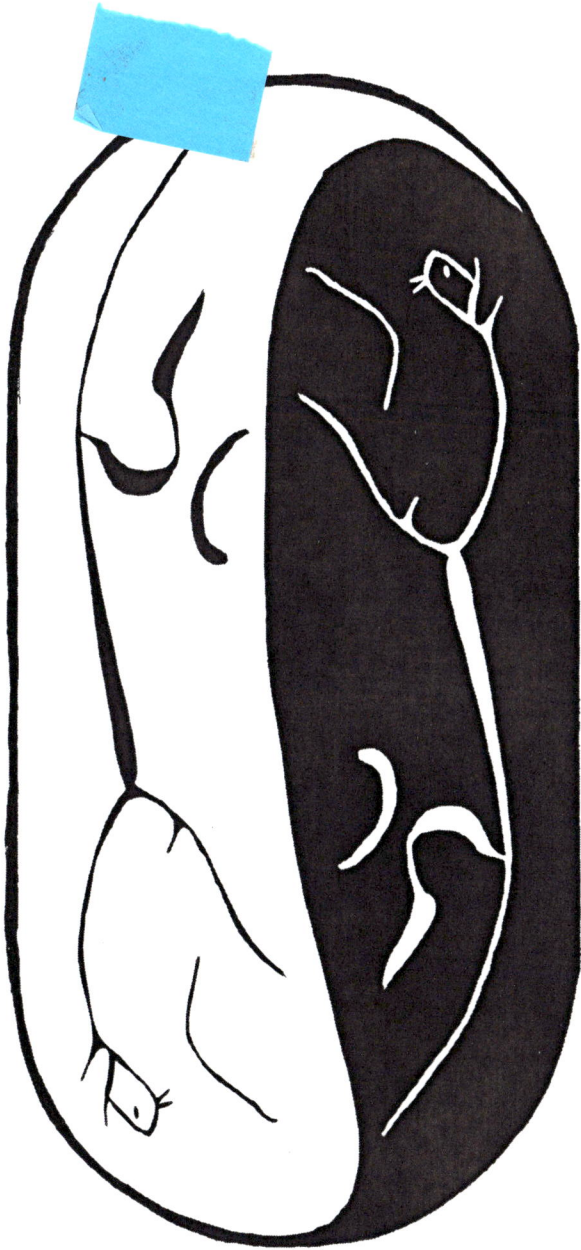

ARE YOU LISTENING HUMANITY?

Are you listening humanity?
I am calling to you.
Awake from your slumber
which has been forced upon you.
I've been calling for centuries
But you've been sound asleep.
Lost in materialism.
Your trance has been deep.

Are you listening humanity?
It is your time to wake up,
from thousands of years sleeping.
You must raise yourself up.
I will ignite your DNA
with the music of love.
To float across space to you.
My gift from above.

Are you listening humanity?
Open your ears to hear,
the sweet notes of the Universe.
They will dissolve all your fear.
The light that's within you
will burst into flame.
United by this love
you will become ONE again.

Are you listening humanity?
I will call long and far.
Till you wake, blessed children,
to the divinity you are.
The truth has been hidden
and kept safe for you.
So that when you awoke
You could find it anew.

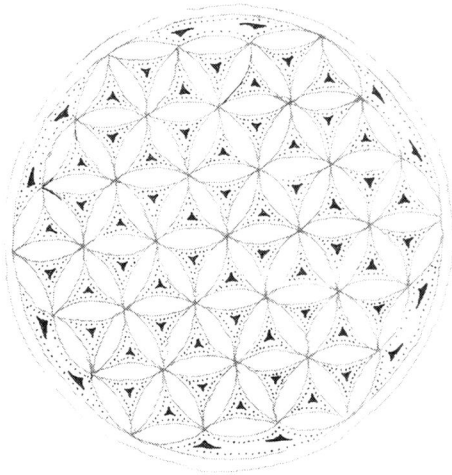

TAKE YOUR HEART FOR A WALK
(Lyrics)

Refrain
Take your heart for a walk.
Take your eyes for a look.
When compassion you feel
Then you'll know what is real.

Overlooking the Thames
by an elaborate cast-iron seat,
stands a woman alone.
Plastic bags by her feet.
All that she has
can be carried in two hands.
Her hair long and dirty,
hangs down in limp strands.

By Waterloo Bridge
in a graffiti daubed subway;
A man clothed in rags
just sits there all day.
His hat set before him
he can watch pennies fall.
If no body throws one
he won't eat at all.

There's a dichotomy
in the area of Leicester Square.
An example of how
materialism isn't fair.
Shops stocked full

of extravagant stuff.
Whilst some have no food
and others not enough.

A man plays his old saxophone.
He has to...to live.
He's nowhere to go
and few people give.
A veteran of war.
He's damaged and broken.
His pain goes unseen,
until humanity has woken.

A young man sits cross-legged
by an Underground station.
For years he has suffered
from love deprivation.
People pass by.
He's no friend in the world.
Except his dog.
Who beside him sleeps curled.

Useless paraphernalia
to tempt human greed.
And yet all around
there's suffering and need.
There are stores full
of expensive and useless clutter.
While the homeless outside
go to sleep in the gutter.

Poverty is all around us
and yet it shouldn't be.

Now we are awakening
it's time for our eyes to see.
These angels of poverty
ignite our spark within.
It is the prompting for our hearts
to let compassion in.

All around London
there are opposite extremes.
Our world's full of abundance.
So why broken dreams?
We can change this tomorrow
Once we choose to see,
That humanity's equal.
And inherently free.

TRANSFORMATION

The spherical egg.
Divinely perfect and smooth.
Catching the sun to caress,
warm and soothe.
Nurturing the tiny creature within.
At any moment to emerge
for a new life to begin.

Nine months of development.
Being comforted and carried.
The human embryo.
Light energy
to manifestation married.
To emerge the perfection
of divine magnificence.
Enabling spirit to embrace
a human experience.

The Caterpillar's world
is too large to comprehend.
Yet its purpose of Being
serves to only one end.
Beyond constantly eating
there is no further vision.
No glimmer of its life purpose
or sacred mission.

A human child emerges.
Divine physical perfection.
Soon lost in the material

and its hypnotic seduction.
The Spirit – all present,
is there all the time.
Patiently waiting for this
beloved light-being to shine.

Change is a constant for
all things that live.
The Caterpillar now prepares
for its own life to give.
The pupae prepared,
it breaks down into goo.
The cells re-arranging to
create something new.

The human can live life
and be spiritually asleep.
Or choose to awaken.
A transformational leap.
Like the pupae...we have
an invitation to change,
into something glorious, colourful.
Of unlimited range.

The imaginal cells
in the pupae present,
the enlightened possibility
not to die...but ascend.
Emerging effortlessly
into beauty and light.
The Butterfly gracefully ascends
to embrace divine flight.

Like the Butterfly
we evolve into Beings of glory.
Yet even that cannot be
the end of the story.
For we are infinite
and immortal Beings of the light.
To awaken we will be
remembering our divinity and might.

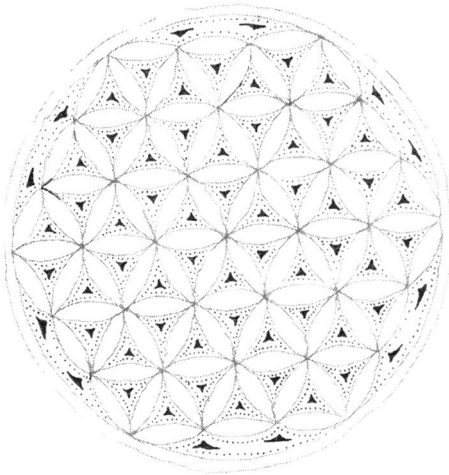

JUST A THOUGHT

A thought is elusive.
One moment it's there; in another it's gone.
Yet the energy it carries
lingers forever on.
A thought is creation.
A seed in the mind.
From whatever its essence
springs the reality for mankind.

If we are sowing with judgement,
resentment and hate,
Then our world suffers the consequence.
Degradation its fate.
Our thoughts are manipulated
by all that we see.
Especially the media, satellite and TV.

They are full of hatred, hopelessness
and so much to fear.
So we think only to worry
for saving all we hold dear.
War seems inevitable.
We think it; so it's real.
A justification for weapons development.
Another arms deal.

Let's switch our minds over
to the channel called LOVE.
And immediately there's help
from the realms up above.
We can vision for ourselves

the World we would see.
Full of harmony and bliss
for all humanity.

We can call upon Angels
to help dream our victory.
Nature's radiant beauty
in land, sky and sea.
I'll hold the vision
and dream it to be.
A paradise on Earth
and humanity free.

TREE OF LIGHT

From the very first moment.
At the second of her birth.
The Tree breathed her light
into the soul of planet Earth.
Her branches extend outward
to the Universe so high.
Reaching beyond human vision
way up in the sky.

Her leaves are the trillions
of heavenly stars.
Beyond all the planets
even Jupiter and Mars.
This highway of starlight
is a divine energy stream.
Brilliant and radiant.
Much more than a dream.

The roots of this cosmic
and light energy Tree
extend deep through the Earth
to touch all land and sea.
The life energy swirls through
the network of roots.
Bursting out at divine places
as sacred spiritual fruits.

All Earth's cosmic portals
and chakra points too
are blessed with light fountains
to help bring in the new.

Love is the light.
Perfect, true and pure.
It will wash and transmute karma
to cleanse and to cure.

The Earth's web of ley lines
will illuminate and glow,
As the light fountain energy
gushes in full flow.
When this love light has flooded
the surface of Earth,
She'll be ready to ascend
and begin her re-birth.

We can assist this by having
the vision to see.
Our Earth healed and beautiful
as we wish her to be.
All humanity united
as we intend love and light.
Our hearts all connected
in our true power and might.

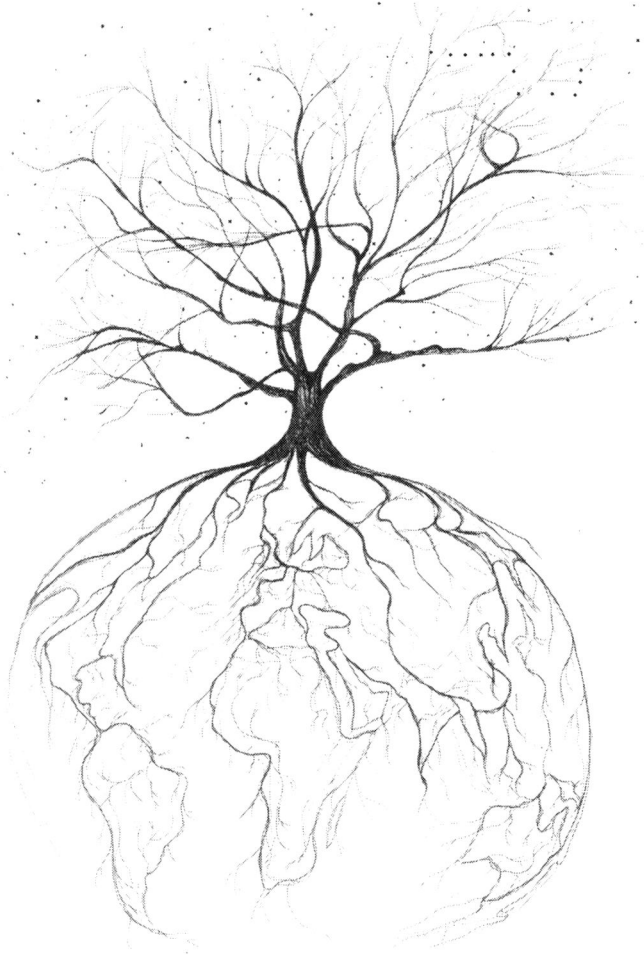

THE UNICORN

A creature of magical grace and light
which stands for all that is good and right.
A seventh dimensional ascended horse.
A frequency of energy. A heavenly force.

For all eternity the Unicorn has sought
To find the heart of purest thought.
To help the World is a selfless desire.
Which lifts human frequency into one that is higher.

The Unicorn is a guide
for enlightened humankind.
A universe in harmony
it will help us to find.
As we attune to ALL nature.
Earth's purest light.
Then paradise will be restored
forever to our sight.

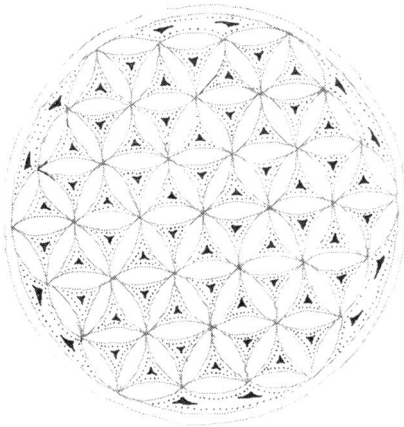

THE RINGING CEDAR

There she stands.
The mighty cedar.
Tall and straight and strong.
She has stood in all her magnificence
For at least ten centuries long.
There are other firs around her
But none as fine as she.
People come from far away
To admire this massive tree.

And when the people have all gone,
The cedars talk amongst themselves.
And with the friends who hear them -
The happy, care-free elves.
Elves laugh and dance
just as they please,
Whilst moving about
amongst the trees.
And singing –
that's what they do best.
For days and weeks
without a rest.

The cedars have elf friends for life
Who teach them all to sing.
By drawing energy from the Earth
so that one day they might 'ring'.
This positive energy harnessed
and held within the wood,
can bless and heal humanity

whose purpose is for good.
To honour and respect
every ancient cedar tree
ensures their gift of love to us
for all eternity.

LOVE IS THE ANSWER

How do we mend the polluted seas?
Especially those around the Florida Keys.
With oil and corexit covering miles around.
Killing the seas creatures. Death without sound.

How do we heal our beloved Earth?
Stop tainting her rivers and appreciate their worth.
Save her forests from ruthless destruction and burning.
Protect the indigenous from murder, annihilation and
hurting.

LOVE is the answer.
Why can't we all see?
If we unite in compassion we'll set the Earth free.
Love passes through water much quicker than light.
Cleansing and purifying all in our sight.

Love heals our wounds and soothes away pain.
From years of complete madness we're made sane
again.
The power of love has no limit at all.
No evil or corruption can withstand, so must fall.

We'll start with our loved ones and closest and nearest.
Reaching out for the World's people
as though they were dearest.
We have the power through our compassion and light,
To transcend the darkness into glory and might.

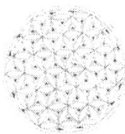

SOLDIERS OF LIGHT

All are of the Oneness
and the Oneness is the all.
When we link arms together
None of us can fall.
We must remember our strength,
our power and our love.
To bring us in tune again
with all that's above.

The soldiers of light
are endless in number
They patiently await us
to wake from our slumber.
When we ask for their help
those Angels unite
To bring us from darkness
back into the light.

We call to the Angels
and Ascended Masters too.
And for all those who speak
for what's blessed and true.
Beloved Archangels
to you we decree
For protection and help
on our quest to be free.

Good creative intention
in our prays and our dreams
will bring about change
far easier than it seems.

When we add in the music
and the love frequency prevails.
We'll attune to the Universe
and the wisdom of whales.

To focus on our God-self
is our primary task.
Help is all around us.
We only have to ask.
Then we'll remember our immortality
and divine connection.
Embracing our Oneness
with compassion and affection.

OH POPPY!

Oh poppy! My heart lifts
when I see your gentle face.
Swaying in the summer breeze
with such elegance and grace.
Often I spy you amongst
the ears of ripened corn.
Like a sea of gold
that scarlet jewels adorn.
Eye-catching in your
vivid, stunning dress.
Delicate as tissue-paper
each petal do I bless.
I am in gratitude.
For you brighten
the dullest day.
Your brilliance splashing colour
when the sky is solemn grey.
But on a sunny day,
when the light reflects your colour,
I am mesmerized by your radiance.
It is unlike any other.

Oh poppy! It is no wonder
that you are the chosen flower,
To adorn our coats in November
when skies are prone to shower.
Your blood-red face a symbol
of all that's good and true.
A prompting to remember
it was in Flanders that you grew.
So I think of all those people

who have died because of war.
Some at home;
but most of them
away on foreign shore.
They will not be forgotten.
And this I say with knowing.
For we wear you, poppy,
proudly to indicate our loving
Of all those souls not here today.
And to whom we send our blessing.
Thank you dearest poppy
for the gift you give by flowering.

SOUL-MATE

We are of the Oneness.
A part of all that is.
Belonging to the cosmic creation
in a frequency of perpetual bliss.

We, who always have been
and together will always be.
Have shared a number of lifetimes.
Souls from the same divine tree.

Soul-mates cannot be separated
no matter how it may seem.
Because regardless of life's changing tides
we swim the same cosmic stream.

The connection between souls crosses boundaries,
Despite all of Earth's stormy weather.
We souls remain linked over aeons.
Love holding us gently together.

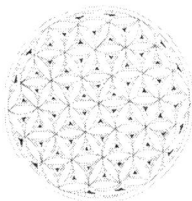

ARCHANGEL MICHAEL

Archangel Michael is of glory and might.
Defender of faith, truth and right.
The protector of all who work for the light.
His blue flame will lead us from out of the night.

Archangel Michael with his sword blazing fire.
Offers us cleansing in his blue sacred pyre.
He can help us create the world we desire.
So humanity can ascend into realms that are higher.

Archangel Michael works on the sacred blue ray.
To bring strength and protection to everyone each day.
A great warrior spirit. To him we can pray.
To fill us with strength. Take hurtful memories away.

Archangel Michael can cut any emotional negative
cord.
When we work for the light, whether here or abroad.
To do decrees will bring us reward.
For he can liberate and protect by using his sword.

Archangel Michael reminds us that we are divine.
As above, so below. The sacred number nine.
When we remember to co-create the perfect design
Of an Earth based on love - wondrous and fine.

LITTLE BULB

The little bulb nestles unseen
in the soil by the apple tree.
It is mid-winter.
There is no sign of life to see.
Sleeping in the arms of nature
it is constantly aware
of weather above ground.
Cold winds, warm or fair.
Snow floats and drifts,
then settles softly,
dusting the earth
with white flakes lightly.
Hidden beneath this virgin blanket
the bulb is in sleep.
Way down below
it is snuggled in deep.
Silent and invisible.
Its very existence unknown,
except to those who
by their hands was sown.
The bulb rests along with
all nature in Winter's death.
To awaken only at the kiss
of Spring's new breath.
When snow retreats
and winds blow warm;
Then does nature's canvass
change its form.
Below the grass
the bulb tentatively awakes.
Green shoots appearing

as the dawn of Spring breaks.
New life begins
where once death was thought.
A re-birth emerges
as from death it is brought.
For a transformation is all that it is.
From one state of being
to a new one like this.
The Sun kisses the Earth
gently warming her skin.
The little bulb responds.
Its new life to begin.
With ecstasy her leaves
thrust into the light.
Keen to escape the coldness of night.
Gently caressing
are the rays of the Sun.
The Winter forgotten.
Jack Frost on the run.
The promise of Summer
beckoning her on.
A flower results
where Earth's blessed sun shone.
Brilliant yellow
to honour the golden sphere.
Welcome dear daffodil.
We give gratitude you are here!

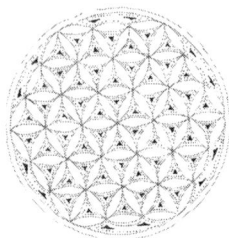

WHALE SONG

We..of the Cetacean ancient elder race..
Speak to you of wisdom,
with loving radiant grace.
Guardians of the Great Whale
and Dolphin Being.
Our desire is to enlighten you
to what you are not seeing.
Our descendants are the light weavers
of the planetary ocean.
In harmony with the sea's
rhythm, heart beat and motion.
Our voices enable the sound
and light threads,
To be woven with love
down to the sea beds.

Each song repeating
the truths of Earth's past;
of the love of the Creator -
eternal and vast.
The music of the Spheres
we weave through the waters.
In celebration of life.
Of all Earth's sons and daughters.
For millions of years
we have blissfully swum,
The blue and green oceans
from when life first begun.
We honour and love our blessed Earth Mother.
And acknowledge her nurturing
of us..and all other.

We bring to her oceans
the Sun's consciousness stream.
Threading through the seas
this life-giving beam.
For we are the musicians
of Earth's watery plane.
Balancing her emotional body
again and again.
Humanity.....what is this
disturbing violation?
The shattering sounds
bringing discordant vibration.
Military sonar tests
emit noises that are disruptive.
It will soon be impossible
for marine life to live.

Our children are haemorrhaging
and, in pain, are dying.
The dolphins and the whales
are grieving and crying.
Oil disasters extinguish
the light from the sea.
The Media stay silent.
So few of you see....
the extent of the disaster.
The pollution. The death.

Wake up humanity
before they snuff out our breath.
The oil industry have air guns.
They exist everywhere.

Pulsing out 200 decibels
of sound without care.

There's nowhere to go.
Nowhere to hide.
You wonder why Whale 'pods'
beached suicidally and died.
And what of the
International Whaling Commission.
To commence legal whaling
they have given permission.
Unlimited harvest
of all the world's oceans.
Hear the cry of the Whales.
The Sea's grieving emotions.
Once love's music is silenced
then chaos will abound.
Should the last Whale sing
the finale of crystalline sound.

The lights will go out.
Yet this need not be.
For you have the power
to break us all free.
No longer be silent.
Speak loud from your heart.
Your apathy and indifference
is why Earth breaks apart.
You are all powerful...
of a spiritually divine kind.
The controllers know this;
that's why they keep you all blind.
Yet you are awakening

*and beginning to seek
The truth in your world.
Perhaps then you will speak.
Condemn the corruption
and restore to the sea,
Harmony and balance
through the LOVE frequency.*

THE SUNFLOWER

*My destiny is to look full on
into the brilliance of the light.
The sun is warm upon me;
caressing gently my golden petals.
I am transformed.
Drinking in hungrily before the coming of night.
And I will watch with vigilance
until the cloak of darkness settles.*

*The light energy stream
from this beacon of consciousness
does not cease,
does not falter – on its journey to my heart.
Many before me received the sun's touch
with happy gratefulness.
Honouring the gift
the light brings for all life to start.*

*Standing strong and tall
with my sundial face,
it is clear how humanity gifted us our name.
Oh we of the planet Earth's plant solar race
are part of the Oneness.
All connected but not the same.*

*I shine brightly,
reflecting the sun's glow.
A reminder to all
of the divine sphere's blessing.
Hundreds of seeds*

from one flower I will throw.
All to become children
to the sun's warm caressing.

Oh you...blessed humanity,
watch me and you'll know
that one small bright light has infinite worth.
Simply cast seeds of love
wherever you should go
and their lights will illuminate
the darkness on Earth.

BEAST OF BURDEN

A beast of burden.
Is that all you see?
Do you really not see
the sentient light that is me?
I am a holder of knowledge.
A 'Don' of my kind.
'Keys' to the Universe dwell
in my heart, soul and mind.
My name is no error.
For in it you'll see the essence of light
in my being....a donkey.

With the body of a horse
I have strength in my back.
It's only the speed
in my legs that I lack.
I am happy to serve you
though I'm regularly abused.
I am over-worked, over-laden
and insensitively used.

My bold shoulder stripe
and short Zebra mane
Are signs of endurance.
Strength to assist, time and again.
But you work me
until I'm dead on my feet.
And sometimes my body
ends up as pet meat.
A vehicle of labour is not
my soul purpose for being.
There is much about me
you simply aren't seeing.

Those ears that you smile at
are a gift to the hearing.
Too large to be mine!
But yet so endearing.
Like two long antennae
they capture the sound
in the energetic field
that exists all around.
I hear the praise
that is sung by all nature,
To the Oneness of everything.
To the divine Creator.

My tail is an asset.
The jewel of my crown.
Like a Lion's,
Its appearance is therefore renown.
It's the representation
of the courage in my heart.
Testament to the creation
in nature of divine art.
Symbolically then,
pinning the Lion's tail on the donkey,
Is true recognition
of the divine status in ME.

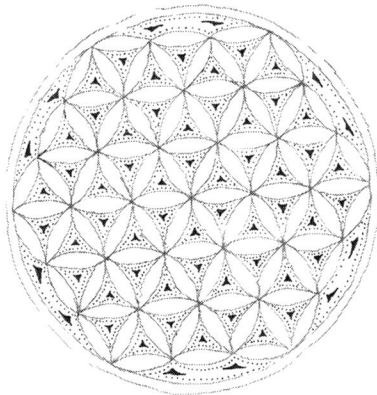

HOW CAN I MAKE A DIFFERENCE?

How can I make a difference?
I am only one small light.
In this world of dense vibration
will I be smothered by the night?
Earth's a place of dark and light
for here exists duality.
Though my light is burning bright,
how can I, alone, help humanity?

Then I remember that from a single voice,
many seeds are sown.
Before too long one little light
has multiplied and grown.
Where once a sea of darkness
stretched beyond where the eye could see.
Tiny lights burst into flame
puncturing through this ebony sea.

For a light of love spreads rapidly
and instantly is catching,
by those whose hearts are open
and minds that are awakening.
Souls of love are moths of peace
attracted to flame and fire.
The blazing brilliance of divine light
which will fan our soul's desire.

Then, uniting our flames together
to make an intensely stronger glow.
Reflecting out like shimmering stars.
A river of light in torrent flow.

No matter how small we think we are,
we need to all recall,
that one small flame in a darkened room
will illuminate wall to wall.

Our work is very simple.
It happens sharing one to one.
Linking souls around the world.
Touching hearts with everyone.
Light attracts more light,
merging into brilliance like the Sun.
The ONE unified light....a beacon,
signals that a new Age has begun.

SOUL GROUP

We've been together, you and I,
over so many lives before.
We have climbed upon mountains.
We have walked along the shore.
We've danced amongst the heavens
looking down upon Earth.
Deciding, together, the time
for our next birth.
We are part of the same
spiritual group of souls.
With shared pathways to Oneness
our unified goal.
Through so many lives
we have chosen to share.
Helping each other grow
with support, love and care.
Oh..we have flown with the angels
across a sun-kissed sky.
Glided amongst Earth's eagles
where we'd soar high and fly.
So many roles have we played
on Earth's emerald stage.
For millennia preparing
for the coming Golden Age.
My friend....I am grateful
for all that we've shared.
Regardless of the lesson.
Whether happy, sad or scared.
Each moment with you
on Earth's roller-coaster ride
fills me with gratitude,
humility and (a little bit) of pride.
As 2012 is with us
I'd like you to know
That I think <u>this</u> life will be
the most spectacular show.

GIVE ME A BREAK

The World's got so crazy.
There's no time to think.
Rushing so much
we hang on the brink
of collapsing exhausted
our energy drained.
Chasing the money
leaves us emotionally strained.

Technology is wonderful but
give me a break.
The constant demand
gives me a head-ache.
Having an email address
isn't enough.
Now they want websites, blogs,
Facebook and all of that stuff.

My mind's in a spin.
I cannot think straight.
However did humanity
get into this state?
Life now revolves around
the mobile phone.
It's as if we're afraid
to go out on our own.

Should someone want me?
Perish the thought
to be non-contactable,
'cos none of us ought!

If we have a few moments..
a rare thing, I know.
Then we're addicted to the TV
and hypnotic Game Show.

What's happening here
is a population sleep-walking.
Hamsters on a wheel
with lives disengaging.
Slaves in a trance.
So our minds keep entraining
enough to stop us
from finally awakening.

What heaven....when we stop
to take a deep breath.
Open our eyes
from this robotic-induced death.
Drink in the energy
from Earth's garden of Eden.
To retrieve our past memories
so deeply hidden.

What of our true ancient history?
Of our 'junk' DNA?
About the spiritual power
we had in past day?
Gifts so incredible
they're like miracles now.
Telekinesis and remote-viewing.
We'll soon remember how.

Once our DNA's reactivated
and considered 'junk' no more,
Telepathy will replace
mobile phones for sure.
Oh, what joy
this will inevitably bring.
We'll have time to dance,
to pray and to sing.

Technology will no longer
be used to control.
We'll be free at last
to embrace heart and soul.
So, I'll take quiet moments
to seek peace within.
Talk to my 'junk'
to encourage its awakenin'!

APPENDIX

Angel Piper
*In the Thistle Chapel of St Giles Cathedral in Edinburgh
there is a wooden carving of an Angel playing the bagpipes.
This, and the healing power of music, as described by Dr Len
Horowitz was the inspiration for this poem.*

A Smile
*If you want proof how infectious laughing is then listen to
'The Laughing Policeman'!*

A Primate Experience
*This poem is in dedication to my late sister, Rowena, who was
a lover of all animals. Her favoured charity being Animal
Aid www.animalaid.org.uk who campaign peacefully against all
forms of animal abuse.*

When All Is Said And Done
Inspired by the Abba tune of the same name.

The New Recruit Soldier
*The book 'The 5 People You Meet In Heaven' by Mitch Albom
is a very thought provoking book but in the chapter 'The
Second Person Eddie Meets in Heaven' on page 59 there is
a paragraph which was part of the inspiration for this poem.
I would also like to give recognition and gratitude for the
work done by those who assist serving and veteran men and
women of the services with issues such as Post Traumatic
Stress Disorder (PTSD). See www.combatstress.org.uk and also
www.ifeal.me.com International Foundation Equine Assisted
Learning which incorporates a 'Dare to Live' program for
those suffering the effects of trauma.
Vaccine mercury genocide is explained on www.drlenhorowitz.com*

The White Lions of Timbavarti

Further information about the sacred white lions and their important role on Earth at this time can be found in the book 'Mystery of the White Lions – children of the Sun God' by Linda Tucker. www.whitelions.org

Heavenly Door of Music

A tribute to the 'Isle of Avalon' and, in particular, to the area of Glastonbury. One of Earth's many sacred places.

The Hidden Story

Is a true story from the area where I live. It is not known what happened to the woman in the poem and whether she still lives or not. But the fact she lived will never be forgotten by me or you, the reader.

Moon Madness

There are a number of sources for alternative information on the Moon.
'Who Built The Moon' is a book by Christopher Knight and Alan Butler.
'Worldbridger' by Juliet and Jiva Carter makes reference to alternative Moon thinking. www.thetemplateorg.com
'Human Race Get Off Your Knees' by David Icke. Chapter 14 is entitled 'Spaceship Moon'. www.davidicke.com

Elsie's Birthday

Elsie represents those elderly people within our society who live alone. During my police service I came across a few like Elsie who also died alone. It always touches the heart with sadness.

The Template
Sacred geometry was the inspiration for this poem. For further reference please see the book 'Worldbridger' by Juliet and Jiva Carter. and the Template ceremonies.
www.thetemplateorg.com

Love Frequency
Solfeggio Healing
Manifestation
Inspired by the work of Dr Len Horowitz and Dr Joseph S. Puleo.
Further information regarding the Solfeggio scale and 528Hz may be found in their book 'Healing Codes for the Biological Apocalypse'.
Also recommended is Dr Len Horowitz's book 'Walk on Water'.
www.drlenhorowitz.com

Who Am I?
Neale Donald Walsch has written two delightful books for children 'The Little Soul And The Sun' (which was the inspiration for this poem) and 'The Little Soul And The Earth'.

Horse Power
'Horse Power' is a tribute to my very dear friend, Natasha, whose love for horses has inspired this poem. She awoke in me the recognition of the sentient and noble essence of the equine Beings. Natasha works in Equine Facilitated Therapy, Energy Healing and Animal Communication. Further information may be found on her website
www.naturalwithhorses.com

Are You Listening Humanity?

Inspired by a beautiful book which helps us to understand who we really are. 'Conversations With God' by Neale Donald Walsch is the best place to start. There are 2 more books in the series. He set up the Conversations with God Foundation www.cwg.org

Take Your Heart For A Walk

In 1974 Ralph McTell's song 'Streets Of London' became famous. I walked the streets of London in 2011 and was shocked to see that nothing had changed. Possibly even worse. Perhaps someone would like to use this poem as lyrics for another thought provoking song?!

Transformation

Very inspirational on the subject of the butterfly's evolution is Elisabet Sahtouris, PhD, Evolutionary Biologist. www.sahtouris.com

The Ringing Cedar

Inspired by The Ringing Cedars series of books by Vladimir Megre about the remarkable Anastasia. www.ringingcedars.com

Love Is The Answer

For more information on the BP Deepwater Horizon incident see www.ianrcrane.co.uk *– 'BP, Population Reduction and The End of an Age'.*

Oh Poppy!
*The illustration for this poem, courtesy of Sophie, features
the regimental badge of the South Wales Borderers. Whilst
the poppies featured represent all of the fallen in war, this
particular badge was chosen in personal honour and respect
for my grandfather, Christopher Albert Norman, who served
in the First World War and retired as Regimental Sergeant
Major in 1935.*

Archangel Michael
*Written in dedication to the work carried out by my dear
friend, Michael Barrette, who hosts an enlightening radio
show and is unfaltering in his commitment to work with
the Archangels and Ascended Masters to bring light to our
beloved Earth and all her sentient Beings. For further
information www.anow.org (for Ascension NOW!) which will
give access to further links.*

Gongs
*Further enquiry into the world of gongs is probably best
started through the work of Gong Master Don Conreaux. His
books 'Gongs of Our Solar System' and 'Magnus Opus of the
Gong' are very informative.*
See his website www.donconreaux.com

Whale Song
*Inspired by Patricia Cori's book 'Before We Leave You'.
About messages from the great whales and dolphin beings.
See www.patriciacori.com.*

How Can I Make A Difference
*Although this poem was inspired by a good friend of mine,
Andy, who asked this question. Many others, like me, I am
sure have asked themselves the same thing. I hope this poem
helps in providing an answer.*

If you would like to know more about Vanessa, please visit her website on www.awakening2011.co.uk.

More information on Vanessa and her books can also be found on www.mvpub.co.uk and on Facebook http://www.facebook.com/MyVoicePublishing

If you liked the poetry here, please like our Facebook page and perhaps review this book on Amazon and leave a comment on Facebook!

Thank you!

Lightning Source UK Ltd.
Milton Keynes UK
UKOW042201140613

212280UK00001B/6/P